One Starry Night In Bethlehem!

Retold by Ada Onwukeme

Illustrated by Elena Paun

Serendipity Press, Jos

"…His Excellence is over Serendipity Press…" Ps. 68:4b"

One Starry Night In Bethlehem!

Published by Serendipity Press, Jos

www.adaonwukeme.com

Copyright © 2020

All rights reserved. No portion of this book may be reproduced in any means without the written permission of the publisher, with the exception of brief excerpts in reviews.

"As a partridge that broods but does not hatch, so is he who gets riches, but not by right; it will leave him in the midst of his days, and at the end a fool." Jeremiah 17:11

One Starry Night In Bethlehem!

Retold by Ada Onwukeme

Illustrated by Elena Paun

Summary: The birth of Jesus Christ from an imaginary perspective of the animals present at the manger.

13-digit ISBN 978-978-36057-8-7

APPRECIATION

This is to thank God, Our Almighty Father, for His enablement to write this book. May He be glorified forever and ever!

DEDICATION

This book is dedicated to the Souls of all Men/Women for their Salvation.

A long, long, long, time ago,

one special starry night in Bethlehem,

Jesus Christ was born as a Baby.

Earlier in the day, things in the town were quite unusual. From sunrise to sunset, donkeys of different shades of color and sizes, were streaming into Bethlehem. Donkeys were everywhere. Some carried women. Some carried children. Some carried men. Some carried loads. Some carried a mix of all the above. All the donkeys I saw had someone or something on its back. Not a single donkey came to town empty.

In the manger, beside an Inn, by the town gate, that starry night a donkey carried a beautiful lady, named Mary. She was expecting a Baby. Joseph, her husband, dropped the donkey off in the manger where the Cow family, the Goat family and I lived.

About an hour later, Joseph and Mary came out. There were no room in the Inn for the them. All the rooms had been taken up.

As Joseph loosened the donkey, for them to leave. Mary said, "Oh My dear Baby Jesus! Baby Jesus! He is coming out!"

Low and behold Mary delivered Baby Jesus! Mary wrapped Him in swaddling clothes.

All the families – the Cows, the Goats, and my family were all fascinated. We all kept peeking to see Baby Jesus.

Few hours past midnight, my former owner Mr. Shepherd came in joyfully with four others. Mr. Shepherd told Mary and Joseph an angel had told them that a Savior has been born. He is the Messiah. The Baby is wrapped in swaddling clothes. Lying in a manger. Lots and lots of heavenly hosts with the Angel were praising God and saying,

"Glory to God in the highest, and on earth peace to those on whom His favor rests."

Shortly after they left in search of the Baby.

with this good news, we were charged with excitement! We older ones were dancing. Our little ones were galloping. We were immeasurably joyful.

As everything calmed down, I remembered the stories Mr. Shepherd sang as he played his harp. One such story was about the Messiah who will come and set people free from the influence of evil.

From what I have seen and heard; I went to Mr. & Mrs. Cow to discuss this thing that has astounded our little community.